W9-BBW-520

PRESENTED BY

Sunny Shuler

in honor of

Gram and Ril.

WESTMINSTER SCHOOLS

Book in
space

2000

David Allen.

SMYTHE GAMBRELL LIBRARY

SMYTHE GAMBRELL LIBRARY
WESTMINSTER SCHOOLS
1424 WEST PACES FERRY RD NW
ATLANTA GEORGIA 30327

ANCIENT GREECE

DISCOVERIES, INVENTIONS & IDEAS

Jane Shuter

Heinemann Library
Des Plaines, Illinois

© 1999 Reed Educational & Professional Publishing
Published by Heinemann Library,
an imprint of Reed Educational & Professional Publishing,
1350 East Touhy Avenue, Suite 240 West
Des Plaines, IL 60018

All rights reserved. No part of this publication may be reproduced or transmitted in any form or by any means, electronic or mechanical, including photocopying, recording, taping, or any information storage and retrieval system, without permission in writing from the publisher.

03 02 01 00 99
10 9 8 7 6 5 4 3 2 1

Library of Congress Cataloging-in-Publication Data

Shuter, Jane.
    Discoveries, Inventions and Ideas / Jane Shuter.
        p.   cm. -- (Ancient Greece)
    Includes bibliographical references and index.
    ISBN 1-57572-739-0
    1. Discoveries in science--Juvenile literature. 2. Greece-
-Civilization--To 146 B.C.--Juvenile literature.   I . Title.
    II. Series: Ancient Greece (Des Plaines, Ill.)
    Q180.55.D57S48 1998
    938--DC21
                                                    98-18189
                                                      CIP

Acknowledgments

The Publishers would like to thank the following for permission to reproduce photographs:
American School of Classical Studies, Athens p. 15 (right); Ancient Art and ARchitecture Collection: pp. 17 (left), 25, 28, R. Sheridan p. 23; Bildarchiv Preussischer Kulturbesitz pp. 27, 29; British Museum pp. 11, 15 (left), 18, 19; Fotograf Nationalmuseet: K. Weiss p. 5; Chris Honeywell p.24; Photo-RMN: Hervé Lewandowski p. 17 (right).

Cover photograph reproduced with permission of the British Museum.

Every effort has been made to contact copyright holders of any material reproduced in this book. Any omissions will be rectified in subsequent printings if notice is given to the Publisher.

Any words appearing in the text in bold, **like this**, are explained in the Glossary.

CONTENTS

Ancient Greece

The Ancient Greeks made many discoveries. Some of them, like their medical discoveries, were passed down to us over time. Others, like the use of steam power, had to be discovered all over again.

Many things the Greeks discovered were just ideas. Few of their inventions and discoveries were used. Ideas mattered more to the Ancient Greeks than putting those ideas to use.

Timeline

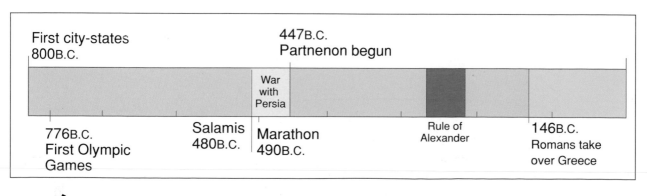

First city-states
800B.C.

447B.C.
Partnenon begun

War with Persia

776B.C.
First Olympic Games

Salamis
480B.C.

Marathon
490B.C.

Rule of Alexander

146B.C.
Romans take over Greece

A Greek man and his **slave**. The Greeks did not make inventions (such as the steam engine) do work for them because there were plenty of slaves to do the work instead.

ARISTOTLE, A PHILOSOPHER, EXPLAINS ANCIENT GREEK THINKING IN ABOUT 350 B.C.:

It is clear that the men who began to think about these things wanted to know things for their own sake, not for any practical use they might make of the knowledge. People did not begin to try to find out about the way things work until they had made themselves comfortable in life. They did it for entertainment.

Ancient Greeks were the first people to think about how people should organize themselves. Greek philosophers wrote about how **city-states** should be run. Their most famous system, in which all **citizens** have a say in how their country is run, is called **democracy**. This word comes from a Greek word "demos" (which means people) and "kratios" (which means power).

DEMOCRACY IN ACTION IN ATHENS

When there was a decision to be made, every male citizen who wanted a say discussed what to do. Anyone was allowed to speak. Then everyone voted on what to do. They also chose **officials** to make sure that **taxes** were paid and laws were kept.

DID EVERYONE HAVE A SAY?

Not everyone had a say in Athens, even though it was a democracy. Women, children, **slaves**, and people who came from other places could not vote, work as an official, or be on a jury.

Decision-making meetings in Athens were held first in the agora, the main public place in the city. A special meeting place, the Pnyx, was later built on a hill outside the town. In this picture of the Pnyx, a decision is being discussed.

Because the Ancient Greeks thought learning was important, they also thought writing everything down was important. At first, they wrote things down by carving stones or writing on wax or clay. Then they used **papyrus** paper from Egypt for paper scrolls or books.

PUBLIC LIBRARIES

It was important to collect information together in one place, such as a library, so people could use it. The Greeks were the first people in the Western world to have libraries that could be used by many people, not just a few **priests** or **scholars**.

ALEXANDRIA

The greatest Greek library was set up in Alexandria, Egypt, in about 290 B.C. It was begun by an Egyptian pharaoh, although most of the scholars who worked in the library and the nearby university were Greek. They were so eager to read as many valuable documents as they could, they bought them, borrowed them to copy, and even stole them!

The library of
Alexandria

The Ancient Greeks loved stories. They wrote stories about gods and goddesses and how they interfered with the lives of ordinary people. They wrote stories about the past, too. They were the first people to write down all of these stories, although they sometimes got real events mixed up with imaginary ones.

MYTHS

The Greek myths are famous. They are stories about the Greek gods. Many of these stories are still told today because they are so exciting. They are full of battles and adventures.

HISTORY

One of the earliest stories written by the Greeks is the *Iliad*, written by Homer in about 700 B.C. The *Iliad* tells the story of Troy, an Ancient Greek city. Some of the story is made up, such as the parts where gods appear. But many people think some of it is true. **Archaeologists** have found evidence of battles in places mentioned in the stories.

Many Greek vases had pictures on them illustrating famous Greek myths. This picture comes from the story of the travels of a hero called Odysseus. The creatures flying around the boat are Sirens. They are singing beautiful songs to lure the sailors to crash onto the rocks. Odysseus has stuffed his sailors' ears with wax so that they cannot hear the songs. He has tied himself to the mast so that he cannot steer the boat onto the rocks.

The Ancient Greeks wrote many books. They also kept lists of who had paid their **taxes**, who had been to court for committing a crime, who had worked as an **official**, and who was a **citizen**. They wrote thousands of official documents.

SECRET MESSAGES

Greek armies had many sneaky ways of sending messages that the enemy could not figure out.

• In about 400 B.C., the Spartans sent messages on long strips of paper. They wound each strip around a wooden rod and wrote the message on it from top to bottom. Then they unwound the paper and filled in the spaces with more letters. If the enemy got the message, they only saw a long strip of paper covered in letters. But when the message got to the right person who had a wooden rod like the one used to write the message, they wrapped the strip around it and read the message.

• In about 170 B.C., a soldier called Polybius used a system of burning torches to send messages. The torches were waved to spell out letters of the alphabet. It was so complicated that the messages had to be short!

An army encampment. Someone is making a record of supplies, another person is reading a secret message, and someone else is sending a torch message.

The Ancient Greeks seem to have been among the first people to see childhood as a separate stage of life that is different from adulthood. Most earlier people seemed to have expected children to learn adult ways as soon as possible.

FUN AND GAMES

Greek babies and toddlers grew up playing many games that children play today. They had rattles and dolls. They had toy soldiers and board games like chess and checkers. As they grew up, boys played early forms of soccer and field hockey.

When boys were about 13 years old and when girls were married (usually between ages 14 and 18), they took their toys to a **temple** and left them as presents for the god or goddess of the temple. They were then grown-ups. Many of their offerings have been found by **archaeologists**.

A vase painting of an Ancient Greek child on a toilet and a photo of a modern child on an Ancient Greek toilet found in Athens.

ARISTOTLE, A GREEK PHILOSOPHER, WROTE ABOUT BRINGING UP CHILDREN IN 350 B.C.:

We give rattles to babies so that, while playing with this, they do not break any of the furniture because young things cannot keep still!

If a boy is to be a good farmer or builder, he should play at farming or at building toy houses, using small tools like the ones that real farmers and builders use.

In Ancient Greece, there were two kinds of medicine. One was partly magical. The other used ideas about keeping healthy and examining patients carefully—ideas that doctors still believe today.

In about 400 B.C., the Greek doctor Hippocrates wrote down the first rules about how to treat a patient (called the Hippocratic Oath) that doctors still follow today. Many Greek doctors used **herbal cures**. Many of the plants they used are still used as medicine now.

MAGICAL MEDICINE

One of the many Greek gods was Asclepios, the god of medicine. Magical medicine was carried out in **temples** to Asclepios, which were built all over Greece. Patients left a present at the temple and slept there for at least one night. Asclepios was supposed to visit them, cure them, and sometimes give them a magical dream, too. The **priests** of the temple also cared for them and often used herbal cures.

Asclepios is treating a patient in a dream in his temple.

This doctor is treating a patient in a clinic. He is taking blood from the patient.

KEEPING HEALTHY

Many doctors believed it was important to keep fit, eat well, and exercise. They said this would stop someone from becoming ill. When patients were ill, doctors gave them herbal cures and kept careful notes on how the cures worked. They tried not to operate. They noticed that people often died after operations from shock, loss of blood, or **infections**.

The Greeks were not the first people to realize that it was important to keep themselves and their towns clean in order to stay healthy. But they were the first people to make sure that there were public **fountains** and bath houses and that the streets were regularly cleared of trash.

CLEAN WATER

Public fountains in Greek towns used pure spring water that had come down from the mountains. People tried not to use water from streams or rivers that might have been **polluted**. The water from public fountains was used for washing clothes and for all cooking and drinking. People also collected rainwater in huge pottery jars, but it did not rain often enough to give them all the water they needed.

These women are getting water from a public fountain.

This is a model of a woman in a bath. Greek baths were not long enough to lie down in.

CLEAN PEOPLE

People were told to wash regularly to stay healthy. Some people with large houses had a washroom at home. They washed from a large pottery bowl on a stand. Some cities also had public baths. These had warm rooms and hot water. They had baths and some of them had showers, too. Some people thought it was weak to go to baths and not wash at home in cold water!

ADVICE ABOUT STAYING HEALTHY WAS WRITTEN BY A DOCTOR IN ABOUT 350 B.C.:

Every day after rising, a man should rub his body with oil. Then he should wash his hands and face with pure water. He should rub his teeth inside and out with peppermint powder to clean them. He should clean his nose and ears with oil.

It does not rain much in Greece, so fresh water is precious. The thinker and inventor, Archimedes, thought of a way to lift water from the river so that it could be used to water crops. This system is still used to lift water out of the Nile River in Egypt today.

THE FIRST FIRE ENGINE

Many Greek inventions were never used, but fire engines were. If they got to the fire fast enough, they were much more efficient than people passing buckets of water.

The first fire engine was designed in about 250 B.C. It was improved by Heron of Alexandria so that the water could be squirted in any direction. Heron lived in the Greek **colony** in Alexandria in Egypt where many **philosophers** and inventors settled to use the big library there. Heron's fire engine was used through Roman times. **Archaeologists** have found the remains of a fire engine in the Roman remains of Silchester, England. It would have been used in about 350 A.D.

A fire engine in action.

MAPS

The Greeks knew that the world was round. In about 290 B.C., the thinker Eratosthenes said it was 24,856 miles (40,000 kilometers) around. He was only off by 42 miles (67 kilometers)! They figured out the lines off **latitude** and **longitude**, which we still use on our maps today.

SKY MAPS

Heracleides drew a map of the planets and put them in their correct order from Earth. He calculated how far away they were, too. His only mistake was that he thought the Sun went around the Earth.

MEASURING TIME

The Greeks used water clocks in which water ran from one pottery jar into another. Athens had a large town water clock. It had a float inside that was joined to a marker outside. This pointed to marks on the outside of the jar that showed the time. Later, water clocks were very complicated. One made in about 270 B.C. used the moving water to ring bells, move small dolls, and even make birds sing.

A mosaic picture of Anaximander. He made a map of the world and invented a sundial to tell time.

PYTHAGORAS

The Greek thinker, Plato, said "God is always doing **geometry**." The Ancient Greeks certainly were. One of the most famous mathematical thinkers was Pythagoras, who calculated many ideas in math that we still use. When you work with shapes and angles, long division, or even more complicated algebra, you are using ideas passed down from the Greeks.

Modern school children still use Pythagoras's mathematical ideas.

THE FIRST COMPUTER?

In about 1900, a Greek ship that had been wrecked was found. It held bronze and marble statues and a pile of cogs and gears with writing on them. Some people thought they were part of a machine that figured out directions. Other people thought they were part of a machine that showed how the planets moved. In 1971, after twenty years of working on the puzzle, a university professor found the answer. It was a complicated machine for calculating the date many years ahead—a very early, simple computer!

Ancient Greek ideas about math and about how to behave were passed down to us in books. But other ideas were lost, either because they were not written down or because the books did not survive. Some writers from the time said things in passing that suggest the Greeks understood the ideas behind jet engines and steam power.

GADGETS

Greek thinkers used many of their ideas to make clever gadgets and toys. They made mechanical toy theaters and magical ink pots that never spilled ink, no matter how you turned them. They thought clever people should not bother to make useful things.

There are some exceptions. Heron of Alexandria used steam power to open heavy brass **temple** doors. This made the temple more magical and mysterious. The Ancient Greeks also made fighting machines, including an early machine gun that fired a row of arrows.

Mines, like the ones these **slaves** are working in, could have been easier to work in with steam engines to pump out the water. But the Greeks did not see why they needed to make slaves comfortable.

EVIDENCE FROM THE TIME

We know what the Ancient Greeks knew from books that were written at the time. These books were copied and passed down. But many books may have been lost, so the Greeks may have understood many more things, We shall never know for sure.

SOMETIMES GREEK WRITERS SAID THINGS THAT GIVE US CLUES. THEY KNEW ABOUT THINGS WE HAVE NO EVIDENCE FOR. WHILE WRITING ABOUT ELEPHANTS, ARISTOTLE ACCIDENTALLY TOLD US ABOUT AN INVENTION FOR DIVERS:

Divers are given breathing instruments so they can draw air from above the water, which lets them stay underwater for a long time. Elephants have trunks that allow them to do just the same thing.

A Greek carving that shows the words and music of an early Greek song of praise to the god Apollo. **Archaeologists** have figured what this would have sounded like.

NEW EVIDENCE

Archaeologists often find new evidence about what the Greeks knew. But they do not always agree upon what the evidence shows! If they only have a few parts of something, they cannot be sure what the whole thing does. Sometimes, even after working on such problems for years, they still cannot be sure.

Vase paintings show us everyday things that the Greeks did not bother to describe in books. This vase shows how they worked metal in a furnace.

GLOSSARY

archaeologists people who dig up and study things left behind from past times

citizens men who are born in a city to parents who were citizens. A citizen had rights in his own city that he would not have in another one.

city-state a city and the surrounding land it controls

colony a place set up in one country by people from another country

democracy running the country by letting the **citizens** make the decisions

fountains places where water is poured out through a pipe

herbal cures medicines and ointments made from plants and herbs

infection something that gets into wounds and makes the patient sick

latitude lines that run east-west drawn across a map or globe to make it more accurate and easier to use

longitude lines that run north-south drawn down a map or globe to make it more accurate and easier to use

officials people who work for the government or state and run the country or city

papyrus reeds that grow near water and the paper that is made by pounding their stalks

philosopher a person who thinks carefully about things and how they work

polluted dirty

priest a person who works in a temple and serves a god or goddess

religious ceremonies special times when people go to one place to pray to a god or goddess

scholars people who study and write books

slaves people who are treated by their owners as property. They can be bought and sold and are not free to leave.

tax a payment that you have to make to whoever is running the country

temple a place where gods and goddesses are worshiped

INDEX

MORE BOOKS TO READ

Baker, Rosalie F. & Charles F. Baker III. *Ancient Greeks: Creating the Classical Tradition.* New York: Oxford University Press, Inc. 1997.

James, Louise. *How We Know about the Greeks.* New York: Peter Bedrick Books, Inc. 1997.

Odijk, Pamela. *The Greeks.* Parsippany, NJ: Silver Burdett Press. 1989.

Terzi , Marinella. *Ancient Greece.* Danbury, CT: Children's Press. 1992.